Dedicated to
the two superheroes in my life: Al and Nick

"Music fills your ears with love."

- Third Grade Student

Copyright © 2016
Written by Lucy A. Warner
Illustrated by Patrick Ackerman
Designed by Jaclyn Alvarado

ISBN 978-0-692-77350-5

Spring Promise Productions LLC
PO Box 558
New York, NY 10021
SpringPromiseProductions@gmail.com
www.SpringPromiseProductions.com

Printed in the United States of America.
Signature Book Printing, www.sbpbooks.com

ZAP! BOOM! POW!

SUPERHEROES OF MUSIC

Twelve Famous Classical Composers with Super Powers!

Written by Lucy A. Warner, M.A.

Illustrated by Patrick Ackerman

EAR READER

Everyone loves a superhero. Well, almost everyone!

What if famous musicians from long ago were really superheroes? What would each one's special power be? In this book, you'll learn some interesting facts about twelve well-known composers. You'll discover a wonderful piece of music each one composed - and what he might have looked like as a superhero!

Inspired by my students, this book is meant for children. Adults are invited, too! Why? Because experiencing music is a fantastic adventure for everyone!

LUCY A. WARNER

TABLE OF CONTENTS...

NTONIO VIVALDI - "V!"

Antonio (ant-toe-knee-oh) Vivaldi (vee-vahl-dee) (1678-1741) had many "V's" in his life! He was born in Venice, Italy, and he was an excellent violinist. For many years, Vivaldi taught music at an all-girls' school in Venice.

Vivaldi had red hair. As a fashionable man back then, he often wore a wig and a red cape. He loved to write music, perform, and travel. Vivaldi composed a beautiful piece called *The Four Seasons*. In this **composition**, each of the four sections is a violin **concerto**, featuring violin with a small **orchestra**. Each **concerto** musically describes a season: spring, summer, fall, and winter.

When he was older, Vivaldi left Italy and spent the last months of his life in another "V" city - Vienna, the capital of Austria.

Vivaldi could play many notes fast and furiously on the violin! Once, a little girl at the school was hiding outside Vivaldi's room, listening. She thought that, on the other side of the door, Vivaldi was a superhero with super fingers and super toes, playing two violins at the same time!

V for Vivaldi
V for the violin
V for Venice
And Vienna, too.

Winter, Spring,
Summer, and Fall
He wrote *The Four Seasons*
For me and you!

LISTEN TO VIVALDI!

Violin Concerto No. 1 in E major, Op. 8 – "Spring" ("La primavera")

GEORGE FRIDERIC HANDEL – "HA!"

George Frideric Handel (1685-1759) was born in Germany, in a city called Halle. What are the first two letters of "Handel" and "Halle?" What are the first two letters of "happy," **"harpsichord"** and "hallelujah?"

Handel played a popular keyboard instrument called the **harpsichord**. When Handel was a young man, he moved to England. Handel composed large musical works called **oratorios**, featuring **orchestra**, singers, and soloists. King George I of England, as well as the English people, were wild about Handel's music!

Handel wrote music for a spectacular, royal fireworks celebration. But his most famous piece is the "Hallelujah Chorus" from his **oratorio** called *Messiah* (Muh-sigh-yuh). In concerts today, when the "Hallelujah Chorus" is performed, sometimes the listeners in the audience are invited to join the peformers onstage and sing with the **chorus**.

If Handel had a superhero voice, his "Ha!" would be heard around the world!

"HA" for Handel
"HA" for the harpsichord
"HA" for Halle,
In Germany.

"HA" for a happy smile
"HA" for "Hallelujah!"
Let's go to London
Sing along with me!

LISTEN TO HANDEL!

"Hallelujah Chorus"
from *Messiah*

OHANN SEBASTIAN BACH – "ZAP!"

Johann (Yo-hann) Sebastian Bach (Bokh) (1685-1750) was born in Germany, in a city called Eisenach (eye-zen-okh). He spent his whole life in Germany. He was a fantastic organist. He also played a smaller keyboard instrument called the **harpsichord**. Bach worked hard many days and nights writing music. His musical hero was a famous, older organ player and **composer** named Dietrich (dee-trikh) Buxtehude (books-tuh-who-duh). This musician lived more than two hundred miles from Bach's house.

When Bach was twenty years old, he walked for ten days just to meet Buxtehude and hear him play! Bach walked on sunny days. On rainy, stormy days, he would find a place to wait inside until the storm was finished and there was no more thunder and no more lightning. One night while he was sleeping, Bach dreamed that he was a superhero with the power to catch an electric bolt of lightning – "Zap!"

Johann Sebastian Bach
Was born in Germany, in Eisenach.
One day he said, "I'll walk for ten days
So I can hear how Buxtehude plays!"

When it rained with lightning,
Bach stayed safely inside.
He met Buxtehude
He walked home with pride.
Organ, harpsichord, black and white keys,
What great music! More Bach, please!

LISTEN TO BACH!

Harpsichord
Concerto No. 1
in D minor

FRANZ JOSEF HAYDN – "HEY!"

Franz (fraw-nts) Josef (yo-zeff) Haydn (hidin') (1732-1809) was born in Austria. He produced the greatest number of symphonies ever written by a single **composer** – over 100! One day, Haydn played a trick on the people who had come to hear Symphony No. 94. When the **orchestra** started to play, the audience enjoyed the soft, short "tiptoe" sounds of the notes. But then, suddenly, the musicians played a very loud chord. It made the listeners jump in their seats! That is why this work is called the *Surprise Symphony*.

What does "p" on a page of musical notes mean? The letter "p" indicates "**piano**" - the Italian word for "soft." This means the musicians should play quietly; "f" means "**forte**" - the Italian word for "loud." Haydn smiled when the **orchestra** played his musical joke on the audience. Can you hear it? Get ready for the loud "**forte**" surprise – "Hey!"

Once, a friend gave Haydn an unusual gift - a talking parrot! What if Haydn were the Superhero King of Soft and Loud? He and his Super Parrot could command all the birds in the world to talk and sing in a soft ("p") or very soft ("pp"- **pianissimo**) or loud ("f") or very loud ("ff" - **fortissimo**) voice - "Hey!"

Dance to the music, tap your toes
Move your arms, jump, then freeze!
Did you know that Haydn composed
Over one hundred symphonies?

Tiptoe softly now with "p"
When "f" comes 'round, get loud!
Haydn winked and smiled happily
When his music surprised the crowd!

LISTEN TO HAYDN!

Symphony No. 94 ("Surprise"), Second Movement

OLFGANG AMADEUS MOZART - "WOW!"

Wolfgang (vollf-gong) **Amadeus** (ah-ma-day-oos) **Mozart** (mo-tsart) **(1756-1791)** was a child genius and a gifted musician. He was born in the country of Austria. When Mozart was very young, he and his older sister Anna Maria (nicknamed Nannerl) went on trips with their father to perform for kings, queens, and other important people. Little Wolfgang Amadeus did tricks playing the violin and the **harpsichord** in crazy, different ways. The royal audience members were so impressed, they exclaimed, "Wow!"

When he grew up, Mozart wrote a beautiful piece for violins and other stringed instruments. In his native language of German, the title is *Eine* (eye-nuh) *Kleine* (kleye-nuh) *Nachtmusik* (nokht-moo-zeek). In English, we call it *A Little Night Music*. One evening, Mozart looked up at the night sky and imagined he was dancing on a magic keyboard, up, up, all the way to the stars, while the **strings** played - "Wow!"

When Mozart was a little boy
Music was his favorite toy.
Kings and queens heard him perform,
His talents caused a musical storm!

He sat backwards to play the keys
He played with a blindfold, he played
on his knees.
Mozart's music - what delight!
You'll enjoy it day and night.

LISTEN TO MOZART!

Serenade No. 13 for
Strings in G major,
First Movement -
"A Little Night Music"
("Eine kleine Nachtmusik")

LUDWIG VAN BEETHOVEN – "BOOM!"

Ludwig (lood-vig) van (fawn) Beethoven (bay-toe-fenn) (1770-1827) was born in the city of Bonn, in Germany. Sometimes, he didn't comb his hair or change his shirt because he was too busy practicing **piano** and writing music! Beethoven composed nine symphonies. In Symphony No. 9, he did something amazing; he wrote music for a large **chorus** of singers to perform with the **orchestra**! (Usually, a symphony is for instruments only.) Even the special **orchestral** kettle drums called "timpani" joined in the music – "Boom!"

If Beethoven had super powers, he would be able to zoom down from the heavens and, while hovering in mid-air, hit the drums with the mallets himself!

In Symphony No. 9, singers perform a wonderful melody set to a type of poem called an ode. The name of the poem is "Ode to Joy." The words tell us we should try to understand and help one another, so that all the people in the world can live happily together.

An ode is a poem
Can you hear the rhyme?
Set it to music,
Keep steady time.

The "Ode to Joy"
Beethoven's ninth symphony
Brotherhood, music,
Singers, timpani!

LISTEN TO BEETHOVEN!

Symphony No. 9, Op. 125,
Fourth Movement

# FRANZ SCHUBERT - "GOTCHA!"

Franz (frahnts) Schubert (shoe-beart) (1797-1828) was born in a little village near Vienna, Austria. He was an excellent pianist. One of his most famous works is a song about a fish called *The Trout*. In German, "the trout" is *Die Forelle* (dee four-elluh). This piece is for one singer accompanied by **piano**. The words and music tell the story of a trout that is happily swimming in a clear, babbling brook. A fisherman steps into the stream. He swirls a stick around in the mud at the bottom of the shallow brook to make the water cloudy, so that the fish cannot see the hook at the end of the fishing line. The fisherman catches the trout - "Gotcha!"

When Schubert finished writing the music for this song, he wondered how it would feel if he had the super power to make water muddy, just by pointing to it! Then, he could take off his glasses. With powerful x-ray vision, he could see through the cloudy water and catch the trout with one swoop of his hand!

Schubert, shoe,
One fish, not two
A trout in a brook
Caught by a hook.

Mud blocks the light
A fisherman's delight
The song will tell
This story well.

LISTEN TO SCHUBERT!

"The Trout"
("Die Forelle")

GIUSEPPE VERDI - "TA-DA!"

Giuseppe (jee-you-sep-pay) Verdi (vair-dee) (1813-1901) was one of Italy's most famous **opera** composers. In Italian, "Giuseppe" means "Joseph" and "Verdi" means "Green." In Verdi's grand **opera** about a princess named Aida (ah-ee-duh), a trumpet march announces soldiers, dancers, slaves, and many other people and animals as they process in a parade, showing off for the king.

One afternoon, after Verdi finished writing the music for all the singers and dancers in *Aida*, he daydreamed that he had the power to fly! He swooped down to hover above the back of a huge elephant that was marching in the *Aida* parade! The elephant was proudly holding a beautiful **brass** trumpet in its trunk. It lifted the trumpet high above its head and made it possible for Verdi to magically blow into the instrument. With his super power, Verdi stayed suspended in the air and played all the right notes without using his hands - "Ta-da!"

Verdi was born in Italy
His name means "Joseph Green."
His opera *Aida* has horses and elephants,
A princess, a king, a queen.

Hear the singing, the trumpet sounds
The big parade starts now!
March to the beat, step with your feet,
Give the king a bow.

LISTEN TO VERDI!

"Triumphal March"
from *Aida*,
Second Act

21

PETER ILYICH TCHAIKOVSKY - "POW!"

Peter Ilyich (ill-yitch) Tchaikovsky (tcheye-cough-ski) (1840-1893) was born in Russia. One day, Tchaikovsky read an amazing tale about a nutcracker soldier who comes to life and meets a girl named Clara. She falls in love with the Nutcracker. Then, a giant Mouse King suddenly appears! He and his soldier mice start to fight the Nutcracker and his army. Clara is worried, but the Nutcracker fights bravely and defeats the Mouse King. The nutcracker soldier turns into a handsome prince, and he and Clara are very happy together. Inspired by this story, Tchaikovsky wrote the music for **ballet** dancers to perform. It is called *The Nutcracker*.

Tchaikovsky also composed music for two more fairytale ballets: *Sleeping Beauty*, about a beautiful princess, and *Swan Lake*, about a magical swan.

One night, Tchaikovsky dreamed that he was the Nutcracker who sprang to life! His super powers enabled him to battle the evil Mouse King and win the fight - "Pow!"

"CHAI" is a tea you drink
"COUGH" is a sound you make
"SKI" down the mountain,
Say "Tchaikovsky" now!

Dance to his three ballets
Sleeping Beauty, *Swan Lake*,
And the famous fairy tale
The Nutcracker - "pow!"

LISTEN TO TCHAIKOVSKY!

"March of the Toy Soldiers" from *The Nutcracker*, Op. 71

ANTONIN DVORAK - "WHOOSH!"

Antonin (an-toe-neen) Dvorak (duh-vor-jhock) (1841-1904) was born in Eastern Europe, in a country called the Czech (check) Republic. He loved his country. He also loved the United States of America. Many years ago, people called America the New World.

One day, Dvorak packed his suitcase and went to live in the United States for three years. During his stay, he wrote a symphony in honor of America. He named the piece the *New World Symphony*. In this work, the musical instrument called the English horn plays a beautiful melody. A friend of Dvorak's thought this melody was so wonderful that he set words to the music. It became the song "Goin' Home." Dvorak's melodies were influenced by American **spirituals** as well as by Czech **folk songs**.

What if Dvorak had superhero powers to fly over the ocean and surf across the waves, traveling back to his country on a magical English horn? "Whoosh!"

Check, checkers, Czech Republic
That's where Dvorak was born
Sing the song called "Goin' Home"
Now, hear it on English horn!

In honor of America
Dvorak wrote this melody
Listen closely, feel it flow
It's the *New World Symphony*!

LISTEN TO DVORAK!

Symphony No. 9 in E minor, Op. 95 ("From the New World)
Second Movement

EDVARD GRIEG – "NO!"

Edvard Grieg (greeg) (1843-1907) is Norway's most famous **composer**. One day he read a play written by a Norwegian writer named Henrik Ibsen. In this exciting drama, a young man named Peer Gynt (Peer means Peter) runs away from home. He travels to many faraway places, experiencing extraordinary adventures. Years later, Peer returns home.

Grieg composed musical pieces to describe each part of the story. Then, he collected some of the pieces into two musical **suites**. You can hear lots of action in each *Peer Gynt Suite*! In one of Peer's adventures, a group of ugly trolls tries to make him marry their princess. They grab Peer, intent on forcing him to live in a cave with them and their mountain king forever. Peer shouts, "No!" and breaks free just in time.

Grieg knew that, if he were a superhero **composer** with special laser eyes, he would come to the rescue and help Peer escape! How? Grieg would yell, "No!" and hum the melody he had written while sending powerful light beams to melt all the trolls!

Can you sing the words in this poem to the music?

Peer Gynt was a boy who roamed
Far away from his home
In a cave he met the trolls
Now they won't let him go.

They demand he spend his life,
Princess Troll as his wife
Dancing, chanting, they surround him
But Peer Gynt says, "No!"

LISTEN TO GRIEG!

Peer Gynt Suite No. 1, Op. 46 – "In the Hall of the Mountain King"

ANUEL DE FALLA — "FIRE!"

Manuel (mahn-well) de Falla (deh feye-yuh) (1876 – 1946) was born in southern Spain. He was an excellent pianist and **composer**. Sometimes he used a walking stick when he strolled around the neighborhood. He had a pet cat named Confucius (con-few-shuss - an ancient Chinese wise man). Much of Falla's music was influenced by the exciting rhythms and sounds of a type of Spanish folk music called **flamenco**. In flamenco, a guitarist plays, a performer sings, and dancers stamp their feet. Sometimes these dancers raise their arms and clap. Sometimes they click rhythms with small, wooden instruments called **castanets** in their hands. Falla's music was famous throughout Spain and many other countries.

Falla wrote music for a **ballet** that describes a story in which gypsies dance around the fire in a ritual or special ceremony, to drive out an annoying ghost. What if Falla's walking stick were a magical, giant **treble clef**? What if Falla could command it to create flames that would drive out evil spirits and ghosts? "Fire!" His cat Confucius could help, too. Now, listen and move to Falla's *Ritual Fire Dance*!

Manuel de Falla of Spain
Thought cats made wonderful pets
He and his kitty loved Spanish music -
Flamenco and castanets!

Falla played the piano
In Spain and England and France
He wrote exciting pieces
Like the *Ritual Fire Dance*.

LISTEN TO FALLA!

"Ritual Fire Dance"
from *The Bewitched Love*
(*El Amor Brujo*)

GLOSSARY

Ballet (bal-lay): A dance form with a history of precise steps and artistic movements, performed to music. Tchaikovsky wrote the music for three ballets: *The Nutcracker*, *Swan Lake*, and *Sleeping Beauty*.

Brass (brass): In a standard classical orchestra, the family of instruments which features trumpet, French horn, trombone, and tuba.

Castanets (kass-tuh-nets): A musical instrument made up of a pair of small wooden "clappers." Flamenco dancers play castanets in their hands to perform rhythmic accents and patterns.

Choir (kwhy-er): A group of singers who perform together as a musical ensemble.

Chorus (core-us): 1. A choir comprised of singers. **2.** The section of a song that repeats in between the different verses of a song.

Composer (kum-po-zer): A person who writes musical pieces.

Composition (kom-po-zishuhn): A musical work or piece. A musical composition can be for instruments or voices or both.

Concerto (kun-chair-toe): A musical work in which one instrument is featured with an orchestra. For example, Vivaldi's *Four Seasons* is a collection of four violin concertos. Sometimes, a concerto can feature two, three, or more instruments.

Ensemble (awn-sawm-bull): A group of musicians who sing or play together as a unified entity.

Flamenco (fluh-meng-koh): A style of music and dance with roots in southern Spain featuring guitar, singing, and dancing. Flamenco dancers use their feet, hands, and castanets as rhythmic instruments. Their facial expressions and hand movements help express the story of the songs.

Folk Song (foke-sawng): A song from a particular culture or region that has been passed down through generations through oral tradition. Some songs written in that style today are also called folk songs.

Forte (for-tay): In music, the letter "f" stands for the Italian word "forte" which means "loud." When a musician is reading music and sees the "f" symbol, this means he or she should play the notes loudly.

Fortissimo (for-tea-see-moh): The letters "ff" indicate "fortissimo" or "very loud."

Harpsichord (harp-see-kord): A keyboard instrument possessing one or more keyboards, with the sound made by pressing a key that triggers the plucking of a string. Harpsichords were very popular during the time of Vivaldi, Bach, Handel, Haydn and Mozart. After the piano was invented, it gradually replaced the popularity of the harpsichord.

Major (may-djer): A type of tonal center or key of a musical composition. Pieces in a major key sound happier than pieces in a minor key. In Schubert's *Die Forelle*, the song starts out in a major key and then, for dramatic effect, shifts to a minor key for a portion of the song.

Minor (my-nerr): A type of tonal center or key of a musical composition. Pieces in a minor key often sound darker or more mysterious than pieces in a major key. Bach's *Harpsichord Concerto No. 1* and Grieg's *In the Hall of the Mountain King* are in minor keys.

Movement (move-mint): One section of a concerto or symphony. Concertos usually have three movements. Symphonies usually have four movements. The abbreviation for "movement" is "mvt."

Opera (op-purr-uh): A musical drama featuring singers accompanied by an orchestra. Operas are staged performances which include sets and costumes. An example of a "grand opera" is Giuseppe Verdi's *Aida*.

Opus (oh-pus): A specific musical work or composition, followed by an identifying number. The abbreviation for "opus" is "op."

Oratorio (or-uh-tore-ee-o): A large musical composition for orchestra, chorus, and featured solo singers. Usually, the theme or subject matter is a Biblical or religious story. Unlike an opera, an oratorio is presented in a concert setting, with no costumes or sets. Handel's *Messiah* is an oratorio.

Orchestra (or-keh-struh): A group of instrument players who perform together as a musical ensemble. In a standard classical orchestra, there are four families of instruments: strings, woodwinds, brass, and percussion.

Percussion (purr-cuh-shun): In a standard classical orchestra, the family of instruments which includes timpani (also called kettle drums), xylophone, castanets, snare drum, triangle, gong, claves, guiro, and many other rhythm instruments.

Pianissimo (pya-knee-see-moh): The letters "pp" indicate "pianissimo" or "very soft."

Piano (pya-no): 1. In music, the letter "p" stands for the Italian word "piano" which means "soft." When a musician is reading music and sees the "p" symbol, this means he or she should play the notes softly. **2.** A keyboard instrument with 88 black and white keys. The original Italian name for this instrument is "fortepiano" because it was the first keyboard that could play notes with loud ("forte") and soft ("piano") dynamics. Before the fortepiano (or piano) was invented, keyboard instruments (such as the harpsichord) could only play notes at one volume, no matter how hard or how lightly the player pressed the keys.

Spiritual (spear-it-chew-ull): A religious-themed type of song developed many years ago by African Americans in the United States.

Strings (stringz): In a standard classical orchestra, the family of instruments which features violin, viola, cello, and double bass. Some other "string" instruments are the harp and guitar. The piano belongs to the string family and to the percussion family.

Suite (sweet): In music, a suite is a collection of pieces which are played in a certain order and which together form one musical composition. (Examples: Tchaikovsky's *Nutcracker Suite* and Grieg's *Peer Gynt Suite*)

Treble clef (treb-buhl kleff): The musical symbol on the five-line musical staff for notation of the middle and high range of pitches. The treble clef, also known as the "G clef," circles around the second line of the staff, indicating the pitch "g."

Woodwinds (wood-windz): In a standard classical orchestra, the family of instruments featuring oboe, English horn, flute, piccolo, clarinet, bass clarinet, bassoon, and contrabassoon.

Violin
(String family)

Trumpet
(Brass family)

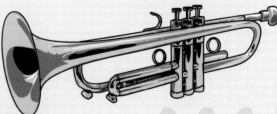

English Horn
(Woodwind family)

Harpsichord
*(String and
Percussion Family)*

Timpani
(Percussion family)

OMPOSER TIMELINE

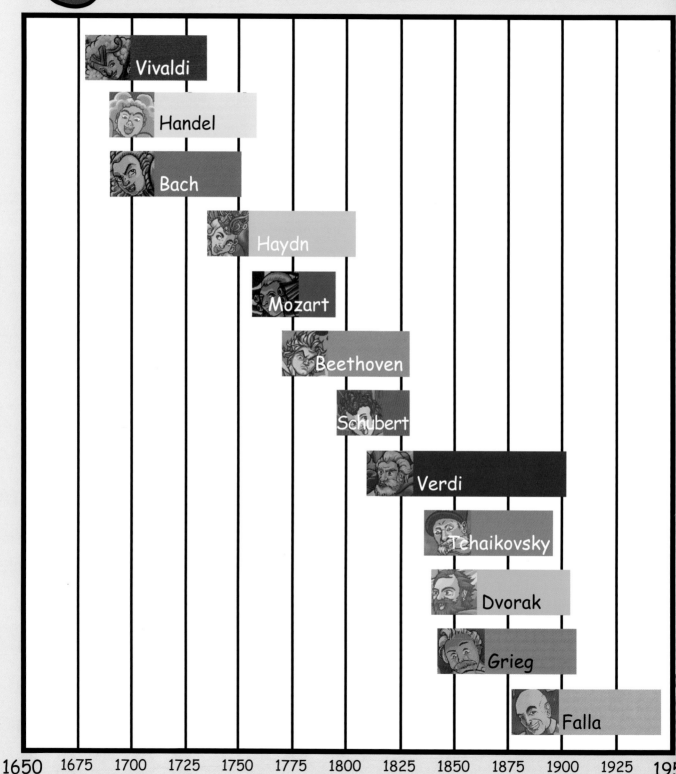

Vivaldi

Handel

Bach

Haydn

Mozart

Beethoven

Schubert

Verdi

Tchaikovsky

Dvorak

Grieg

Falla

1650   1675   1700   1725   1750   1775   1800   1825   1850   1875   1900   1925   195

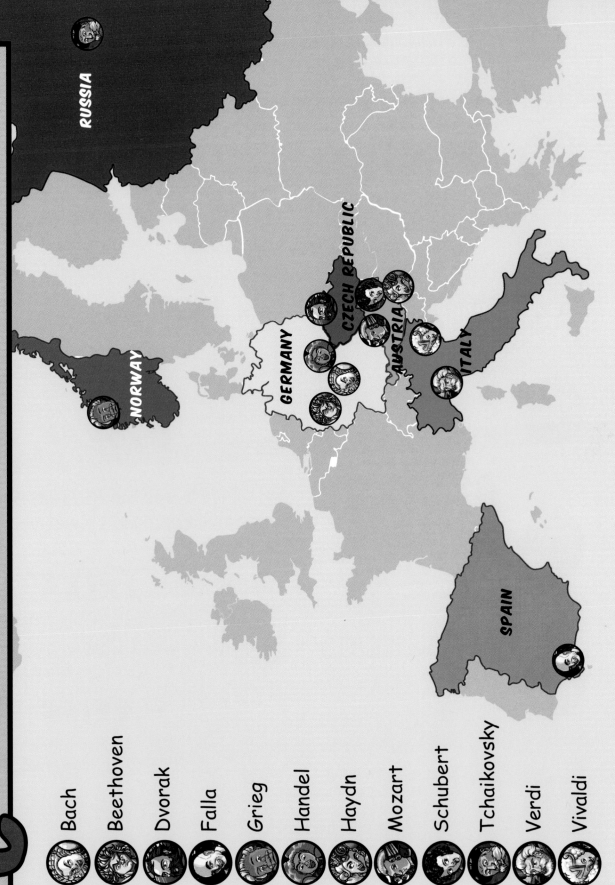

COMPOSER MAP

RUSSIA

NORWAY

CZECH REPUBLIC

GERMANY

AUSTRIA

ITALY

SPAIN

Bach

Beethoven

Dvorak

Falla

Grieg

Handel

Haydn

Mozart

Schubert

Tchaikovsky

Verdi

Vivaldi

OMPOSER QUOTES

 "There is nothing to it. You only have to hit the right notes at the right time and the instrument plays itself."

- J.S. BACH

 "From the heart . . . may my music find its way to the heart."

- BEETHOVEN

 "My own duty as a teacher is to give what encouragement I can to the young musicians of America."

- DVORAK

 "In my very early childhood, when I was only two or three years old, my babysitter's songs, dances, and stories opened gateways to a magical world."

- FALLA

 "My imagination is rarely as active as when I am writing to a friend!"

- GRIEG

 "I should be sorry if I only entertained them; I wished to make them better."

- HANDEL

"Often when I was wrestling with obstacles of every kind, when my physical and mental strength alike were running low and it was hard for me to persevere in the path on which I had set my feet, a secret feeling within me whispered: 'Perhaps your work may, someday, become a spring from which tired people may draw a few moments of rest and refreshment.' And that was a powerful motive for pressing onward."

- HAYDN

"Melody is the very essence of music. When I think of a good melodist, I think of a fine racehorse."

- MOZART

"I try to decorate life with my imagination as much as I can."

- SCHUBERT

"Music's triumphant power reveals to us beauties we find nowhere else."

- TCHAIKOVSKY

"If others say: 'He should have done thus and thus,' I answer: 'That may well be so, but what I have done is the best I can do.'"

- VERDI

"The festive Spring has arrived. The birds celebrate her return with happy songs."

- VIVALDI

QUESTIONS

1. Franz Schubert wrote a famous song about a fish. What kind of fish is it?

2. In Ludwig van Beethoven's Symphony No. 9, the kettle drums play with the other instruments in the orchestra. What is another name for kettle drums?

3. In what country was Edvard Grieg born?

4. What instrument was chosen by Antonin Dvorak to play the beautiful melody in the second movement of his *New World Symphony*?

5. Which classical composer was a child genius who traveled and performed tricks on the violin and harpsichord for many important people, when he was just a little boy?

6. What kind of animal did Manuel de Falla have as a pet?

7. What is the name of Antonio Vivaldi's well-known piece that describes nature?

8. What is the name of the great organist and composer whom Johann Sebastian Bach walked over 200 miles to meet?

9. Peter Ilyich Tchaikovsky wrote the music for three ballets. What are the names of these ballets?

10. Is George Frideric Handel's *Messiah* an opera, an oratorio, or a symphony?

11. Which Italian composer wrote the music for the opera *Aida*?

12. What is the special name for Franz Josef Haydn's Symphony No. 94?

ANSWERS

1. Trout 2. Timpani 3. Norway 4. English horn 5. Wolfgang Amadeus Mozart 6. Cat 7. *The Four Seasons* 8. Dietrich Buxtehude 9. *Nutcracker, Sleeping Beauty, Swan Lake* 10. Oratorio 11. Giuseppe Verdi 12. Surprise Symphony

LISTENING/VIEWING GUIDE

VIVALDI (p. 6) - Violin Concerto No. 1 in E major: "Spring" from The Four Seasons
https://www.youtube.com/watch?v=TKthRw4KjEg
https://www.youtube.com/watch?v=aFHPRiOZeXE

HANDEL (p. 8) – "Hallelujah Chorus" from Messiah
https://www.youtube.com/watch?v=VI6dsMeABpU
https://www.youtube.com/watch?v=7YaGwI7GjlA

J.S. BACH (p. 10) – Harpsichord Concerto No. 1 in D minor
https://www.youtube.com/watch?v=rsaIW5MrbMc
https://www.youtube.com/watch?v=sGHgLvb5PYE

HAYDN (p. 12) - Symphony No. 94 ("Surprise"), Second Mvt.
https://www.youtube.com/watch?v=eVXalu0p1wo [start 9:37]
https://www.youtube.com/watch?v=hnv1ZBBRBcc

MOZART (p. 14) – Serenade No. 13 for Strings in G major, First Mvt. – "A Little Night Music" ("Eine Kleine Nachtmusik")
https://www.youtube.com/watch?v=Qb_jQBgzU-I
https://www.youtube.com/watch?v=FTgvh7moqQM

BEETHOVEN (p. 16) – Symphony No. 9, Op. 125, Fourth Mvt. – "Ode to Joy"
https://www.youtube.com/watch?v=a97EG7Mqp8g
https://www.youtube.com/watch?v=kbJcQYVtZMo

SCHUBERT (p. 18) – "The Trout" ("Die Forelle")
https://www.youtube.com/watch?v=NF9DrUXowBo
https://www.youtube.com/watch?v=k20qXLp-aS8 [start 4:40]

VERDI –(p. 20) – "Triumphal March" from Aida, Second Act
https://www.youtube.com/watch?v=l3w4I-KElxQ
https://www.youtube.com/watch?v=AssDQbaIP_I [start 2:31]

TCHAIKOVSKY (p. 22) – "March of the Toy Soldiers" from The Nutcracker, Op. 71
https://www.youtube.com/watch?v=LmlEmi2HxjY
https://www.youtube.com/watch?v=2AUMARqt8eY

DVORAK (p. 24) – Symphony No. 9 in Em, Op. 95, ("From the New World"), Second Mvt.
https://www.youtube.com/watch?v=aYl4Xb4cDQ8
https://www.youtube.com/watch?v=H1lF9D0zasY

GRIEG (p. 26) – "In the Hall of the Mountain King" from Peer Gynt Suite No. 1, Op. 46
https://www.youtube.com/watch?v=PBsFYKzhk5E
https://www.youtube.com/watch?v=uwKfTk4cVqQ

FALLA (p. 28) – "Ritual Fire Dance" from The Bewitched Love (El Amor Brujo)
https://www.youtube.com/watch?v=auRUxPPqDcQ
https://www.youtube.com/watch?v=McDd1xWjt78

BIBLIOGRAPHY

Benestad, Finn and William H. Halverson, eds. Edvard Grieg: Letters to Colleagues and Friends. Columbus, OH: Peer Gynt Press, 2000. Print.

Biography.com Editors. Giuseppe Verdi Biography. A&E Television Networks. Biography. Web. 25 July 2016

Dvorak, Antonin with Edward Emerson, Jr. "Music in America." Feb. 1895. Artsinteractive. Web. 8 Aug. 2016

Flower, Newman. Franz Schubert – The Man and his Circle. New York: Tudor Publishing, 1935. Archive.org. Web. 5 Aug. 2016

Harper, Nancy Lee. Manuel de Falla: His Life and Music. Lanham, MD: Scarecrow Press, Inc., 2005. Books.google. Web. 3 Aug. 2016

Machlis, Joseph and Kristine Forney. The Enjoyment of Music. New York: Norton, 7th ed., 1995. Print.

Spanoudis, S. L. "Poet's Corner: Le Quattro Stagione (The Four Seasons). theotherpages.org. 2009. Web. 9 Aug. 2016 [Note: Vivaldi possibly wrote the "Spring" sonnet]

Watson, Derek. Introduction. The Wordsworth Dictionary of Musical Quotations. Hertfordshire: Wordsworth Editions, Ltd., 1994. Print.

ABOUT THE AUTHOR

Lucy A. Warner (B. M. Ed., M.A.) is a graduate of the University of Texas (Austin) and Eastman School of Music (Rochester, NY). She studied music education, music history and performance practices, theory, voice, piano, and harpsichord.

Ms. Warner began teaching in San Antonio, Texas, earning the Teacher of the Year award in her third year instructing students at Wilshire Elementary School. She then moved to Richmond, Virginia, where she worked with both elementary and Middle School-aged children in the inner city.

Preparing to bring fruits of the musical world to students, the author learned to play guitar and embarked on a career of performing, composing, and touring. Her musical styles included Broadway, pop, rock, country, ethnic, swing . . .

Ms. Warner brought her professional experiences to The Browning School in New York City in 2001, where she has taught music to elementary school students for over fifteen years. ZAP! BOOM! POW! grows out of the popularity of the Composer of the Month program which she initiated in the classroom. Seeing how children are energized as they learn about the lives and musical achievements of the world's most famous musicians – from Bach to Stevie Wonder, to today's brightest stars – the author was inspired to present twelve classical composers in her first book – while adding a surprising, new dimension.

ZAP! BOOM! POW! jolts famous musicians to life – as superheroes!

Ms. Warner recommends this book for children, parents, teachers, all music-loving adults, and for reading to pets – including her two cats Vivaldi and Missy.

ABOUT THE ILLUSTRATOR

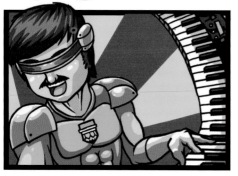

Patrick Ackerman is an illustrator/pixel artist who graduated from The School of Visual Arts with a BFA Illustration in 2010. With degree in hand, Pat marched forward through the world of retail . . . until he was swept away into the world of video game development and polished his pixel art skills for years to come.

Music influences Pat on a daily basis, and he's even been spotted playing synth and drums for different musical endeavors throughout his life. Illustrating famous musicians for this book, and connecting each artist with a superhuman power, brought "a great new perspective" to his understanding of each composer. Currently, Pat can be seen in dark rooms, pumping out pixel art for his new video game that he's co-developing with his best friend.